" We all want to know that
our life meant something,
And that we did something
for someone else
and that we spread
positivity,
no matter how big
or how small"

- Beyoncé

Unspoken Monologues: A Journey to equality

Volume 1

Michael Landreth

To everyone with a story

Table of Contents

Unspoken Monologues:
A Journey to equality

The *unspoken monologues* is a collection of stories that have been stifled and silenced due to feelings of disgrace, shame, and for fear of speaking out. We share these stories to give a voice to our LGBTQ friends and our shared community. These stories are directly inspired by people's own experiences—ranging from hardships to times of pure happiness, from bullying to transitioning, from coming out to starting a family, and even marriage.

Speak Out

That's so GAY!
Faggot
My son is gay
Two men cannot raise a child
It's my fault!
What did I do wrong?!
He just wants to be a girl
I'm Alone
It was the happiest moment of my life
It's not a choice
What is wrong with me!?
I'm Gay
I finally will feel right.
It's some thing I can't explain
She's just a slut
It was nothing I did wrong

All these statements have been said by or to any number of the LGBTQA community.

These monologues are for those who have never told their stories.
These monologues are for those who aren't here.
These monologues are for the gays.
These monologues are for the lesbians.
These monologues are for the queers.
These monologues are for the allies.
These monologues are for US!
These monologues are the unspoken monologues.

It was nothing I did wrong

Coming out is not only one person's journey. It takes time for each person in their life to come out and either accept it, take time to digest it or discontinue the relationships with the person who came out.

My son came out last year to his siblings and me.
My first thought was what did I do wrong.
After talking to my son it was nothing I did wrong.
I always thought my son would marry a beautiful woman
And have my grand children.

When he came out
A part of me needed time to digest what had happened.
I thought about how marriage is not legal for same sex couples,
I thought about bullying,
I thought about AIDS,
Children are not an option,
I even nearly buried the thought of grandchildren from him.

I was scared for him
Because being gay isn't accepted in our society.

It has changed since I was a child
But I was worried about how our culture is.
Another thing that came to my mind was the AIDS epidemic
I had a friend from high school and a cousin die from AIDS.
I would not be able to handle losing my son to AIDS.
I love my son no matter what
But some of these things worry me.

I am worried for my son being gay.
I want what is best for him.
He seems happier that he came out
And I guess that all I can say to him is that I still love him.
I raised my son to be smart and responsible.
I accept him and love him
No matter who he loves.

That's so GAY Fact #1

28% of LGBT youth
Drop out of school
Due to harassment

-GLSEN Gay, Lesbian, Straight education network

I won't parade it around then

High school is a time of finding one's self and determining what an individual would like to do after. In high school some students come out and are accepted by their peers, while others are harassed because their sexual orientation or gender identity.

It happened again.
I was in school and just looking outside, when I saw him.
He is so cute.
He's a senior so he didn't have to get to school until his class around 3rd period.
We had class together, well kind of…
He was the teacher's assistant in my theatre class.
He is so dreamy.
Of course, he isn't gay
But I can look right?

Well class finished, and I was walking in the hallway,
Went to the bathroom during passing period,
And there was a bunch of guys in there.
I did my business and kept to my own
One of them said, "There goes that little faggot".
I didn't pay attention to it.
I tried to leave when another asked if I wanted to suck him off.
I didn't want to.
Passing period was almost over, I tried to leave.
They grabbed my backpack and pushed me around
I heard the bell ring in the hall.
I thought, "Great, now I'm late to class".

I just wanted to leave this bathroom.
I stood up and got my backpack
They took their time to give it to me.

I went to class late
Got a detention for being tardy.
I took the detention
I was too scared to tell what happened to me
And why I was late.
It's embarrassing.
It's my first detention.
It will be ok.

A couple days later,
I ask to talk to my teacher about the detention
He said he would let me talk to him.
I told him what happened.
I didn't know the guys' names
My teacher said if I didn't "parade" myself around school being
gay
Things like this wouldn't happen.
I told him I would try to not "parade" it around.
It made me feel more embarrassed,
Running for help.

I haven't told my mom this happened
I lied and said I had to stay after to work on a project.
My parents aren't together anymore.
I hide my sexuality at home
And usually stay quiet.
I think my mom knows

But she doesn't say anything about it.

My dad,
I know I will never say that I'm gay to him.
When California passed the law banning gay marriage under
Proposition 8 my dad said,
"Good those people don't deserve the right to ruin marriage."
My dad comments on how gay people are an abomination
And should not have rights.
From hearing those words
I feel as though I will never tell him.
I'm alone in this fight.

That's so GAY Fact #2

90% of LGBT students
Hear anti-LGBT
Comments in school

On average,
An LGBT high school student
Will hear 26 anti-LGBT slurs
Per day

1 out of 3
Will be from
A school staff member

-GLSEN Gay, Lesbian, Straight education network

MMM...look at that ass

And sometimes coming out is a time you think will go bad but it goes surprisingly well.

My dad and I have never really seen eye to eye,
We're just the complete opposite of each other.
He works construction and I...
Well I do theatre.
I've always tried my best to get along with him,
I'll never forget.

One day I was just hanging around the house
My dad came home from work.
I was pretty bored
So I decided to strike up a conversation,
It was actually going pretty well
He sat down and started watching a football game,
I decided to join him
Even though I'm not a big fan.
There was the blue and white team against
the green and yellow team.
I had no clue what was happening
When they said third down I was clueless.
But i guess my dad's team was losing
He was yelling at the defense.
We were talking about school and work
And even theatre because I had a show coming up in a couple
weeks
We were just watching football together
It was nice to have somewhat of a bond going

I kinda forgot who I was hanging out with.
Then all of a sudden
The camera zooms in on one of the cheerleaders....
Then on a cheerleaders butt,
And my dad says "Mmm…Look at that ass,"
While nudging me,
Trying to find some common ground.
I smiled and nodded
Playing it cool then all of a sudden
The camera zooms in on one of the football players
The next shot was up close up
On a football players butt...
And then without even thinking of who I was talking to
I said "Mmm look at THAT ass."
I realized what I had just said
Tried to play it off with a giggle.
My dad looked at me in shock
He was definitely not laughing.
I silently got up and walked to my room embarrassed.
After about 10 minutes my dad knocked on my door
He told me he had known for a while and was waiting on me to
say it.
He also said it was okay and he still loved me.
And that's when my dad found out I was gay.

My Partner is HIV Positive

Knowing someone's status is very important because HIV and other STIs are on the rise. Even knowing status is a preventative to passing the virus. Get yourself tested if you don't know your status

When I first found out he was positive
You could understand that it's quite emotional
What if I got it?
It doesn't change how much I like him.
We were together for a year and I feel as though I actually knew him
Before we got serious and were sexually active.
Being with him each day is a gift
Because each day to him is a gift
Because he can die tomorrow or in a year.
For us its just taking each precaution to make sure I am safe
And he is safe.
I know that it's a lot to talk about
But us knowing he is positive and I am negative is a difficult conversation
And a difficult relationship to have
But it is not a death sentence anymore.
Every day he takes his meds and is as healthy as he can be each day.
His meds do take a lot out of him
He takes them every night
And after he takes them he has about 20 minutes
Before he crashes completely.
And even with his meds there is so much to worry about

Because if I get a cold I can get over it
But if he gets the same cold he is out of work for a while
Because it hits him harder, because his immune system isn't as strong
It's a good thing that he got a health insurance policy before he became positive
Because most companies will deny a policy on the basis of being HIV+
I never told my family
And never will tell my family that Chris was positive because they are scared that I will die of AIDS.
I know its just family being concerned for me
But we were happy.
I would go with Chris to doctor appointments
And hear from the doctor about how he is doing.
And I get tested monthly
To insure that I am safe along with him.
I, to this day am negative.
We are not together anymore but
Chris is healthy
Or he was the last time I heard from him.

Memorial: Blazing the Trail

When asked who the most influential person in the LGBT
community everyone has that person who is their hero.
Here are a few heroes.

Ellen is a huge inspiration for everyone.
She's strong, supportive,
And she's made it by herself.
Even through all the hard times and trouble
She has persevered
And she really cares that other people do the same.
I think Ellen is an amazing person,
Because she didn't let the fact that
She is a lesbian and woman
Get in the way of making a name for herself in television.
And I respect all women who don't let society get in the way of
their dreams.

Lady Gaga,
Not because she is the most recent and a huge celebrity,
But because she helped the current push for the acceptance of all
gay people.
All her work with her Born This Way Foundation
And incorporating a positive self image
With the Body Revolution 2013 campaign
When she opened up about her own eating disorder.
Along with launching the Born Brave bus,
Which will be traveling with her 2013 tour
Offering counseling and help
To those who are born brave.

Neil Patrick Harris
Not just because he's hot and gay,
But he is one of those lucky people actually living his dream.
Not only does he have a career doing what he loves,

But he also has created a beautiful family
And life for himself.
He is an incredible role model
To those who are gay and straight.
He proves that being a gay parent isn't bad
And shows nothing but love for his two children
And husband.
His positive outlook and passion for gay rights is truly
Inspiring.
He is a great role model for what a LGBT family can be.

Sharon Needles/Aaron Cody.
Because she has broken many of the
Traditional looks of the gay community.
People often see us as high maintenance
And only focused on improving ourselves
For sexual pleasures,
But Sharon has been able to take people's attention
By her art form
And made them see
What the other half of our community is all about.
She uses drag as a weapon
When others use it to make a lifestyle.
It's basically like being a painter
And using art
To show people a different word.
Winning RuPaul's Drag Race has given her the tools
To truly expand that mindset.
Some people don't understand it,
But those that do appreciate her form of expression.

Lieutenant Dan Choi was one of the leaders for the repeal of
DADT
He was a graduate from West Point.
He then served as an infantry officer in the army.

He was discharged after his coming out.
He then wrote a letter to President Obama and Congress
He showed me that a single person
Can start making a difference
After being discharged he became an activist
He now speaks at many gay rights events
He got what was right.
Don't Ask Don't Tell was repelled.
He is a hero to me.

I almost ended it all

Since I was younger I always knew I was different.
I knew I liked boys
And that was not right.

I come from a family that tells me that
It is not normal.
The community I grew up in told me
It was the wrong kind of love.

I went to church to pray to God
To take the gay thoughts out of my head.
I asked and begged to be straight.
After weeks of begging and asking
I knew nothing was going to happen.

I made a plan.

My family didn't accept me for being gay.
They didn't kick me out, but they never acknowledged it.

I decided it was time to handle this problem.
I went to a local McDonalds and wrote a suicide note.

I was used to taking the train at night,
I knew the platform would be empty.

In the letter I told my parents exactly what I was thinking.
I told them that I was sick of being a burden to them
I told them that I was sorry that I let them down

And I'm not the son they wanted.

I walked downstairs to the platform.
I let the A train go by
I knew that the B train didn't stop here.
I was ready to be free from this problem.

I pulled the letter out of my backpack,
Placed my backpack on the bench
And placed the note on the top of it.
I tried to not think of anything except jumping.

Just as the train began approaching
The platform began rumbling,
I saw an older man walking down the stairs.
He was wearing a long black jacket,
That jacket reminded me of
My grandfather's jacket he would wear, when he visited.

The man stared at me the way animals stare at each other.
I don't know why he wouldn't look away
All I know is that because he didn't, I am still here.

I will never be able to thank him.
I never knew his name or his story
But the way he looked at me kept me
From stepping in front of the train and
Ending it all.

Years later I realize that just because I am gay,
Does not mean that I am unlovable.

It took a while for my family to come around
But they realized that there wasn't a difference
Between who I was born and who I am now.

The first time I felt that love was
When I went out to dinner with my family
After my freshman year of college.
My father said that he was happy that I'm alive
And that he can put his arm around me
And kiss me on my head.

"Corrective" Rape

First identified in South Africa corrective rape has and still is sometimes used because an individual has gone against the social norm of being heterosexual. Both homosexual men and women have been raped by their opposite sex to "correct" them.

In my country being homosexual is not accepted
Not like it is in America.
When I was younger and told my family
I was in love with a woman.
They didn't take it well

I was sent to away
And put through the worst experience of my life.

They gave me electric shock therapy
To get the homosexual tendencies out of my head.
After weeks of this painful "treatment"
They changed their tactics,
Something they said to be more effective.

I was raped as a corrective therapy.
For weeks I was locked in a room
That was like being in prison.
Cold and dark

Every day I would get a meal
Then a few hours later two to three men would enter my room.
They would rape me repeatedly.
When it happened all I could do was scream

Beg for it to stop,
But I knew it would never stop,
It hurt.

I screamed for help
But my screams went nowhere,
No one came to help me.
I was alone.

I have since then left my home country with my partner, to find a
better life than in my home country.

That's so GAY Fact #3

26% of LGBT youth
Are forced to leave home
Because of conflicts with family
Over sexual orientation
And/or gender identity

-Lambda Legal

The back up plan

While some people think suicide is an answer, some keep it a secret for a fear of rejection but, in time come out to their loved ones.

I just told my mom that I'm gay.
I sat her down and the first thing I said was,
"Will you be my mother no matter what?"
She said "yes"
I asked her
"Even if something was wrong with me?"
She was worried
She said, "Yes what's wrong?"
I felt the tears welling up in my eyes.
I told her that I am in love with someone.
She looked concerned about where this was going
But she smiled and asked,
"What's her name?"
I smiled and told her how amazing this person is.
She smiled.
She probably thought that she was pregnant.
I told her, "His name is Kyle."
She looked confused and said
"That it was an interesting name for a girl."
I laughed and said,
"HIS name is Kyle."
I said, " Mom, I'm gay."
She gave me a hug and asked
"What do you think is wrong with you?"
We both laughed and smiled

She asked if she could meet him.

I laughed and told her that he was outside in his car
In case things went bad.
She laughed and told me to invite him in.
I went outside wiping the tears from my eyes
I got in the car and gave him a hug and kissed him.
I told him that I told her and he smiled at me
I told him to get out of the car
That she wanted to meet him.

I brought him into the house and my mom gave him a hug.
We all laughed with our faces drenched in tears.
She asked how long we had been together
Hesitantly I told her that we had been together for 3 years and 2
months.
Shocked, my mom smiled
She told him, "Well I guess you're basically part of the family."
My mom asked if she could talk to him alone.
She took him into her room.

I went to grab my sister from upstairs,
She already knew Kyle
We always picked her up from school.
I told her that I told mom.
We came down together
My mom and Kyle were on the couch laughing
My sister ran over to Kyle and gave him a big hug.
My mom was shocked to find that my sister had known about
him.
My mom asked if she was the last one I came out to

I told her yes.
I met Kyle's parents after our one-year anniversary.
She smiled and asked my little sister if she liked Kyle
She said, "I love uncle Kyle"
When we heard that we all laughed
And smiled.
And my mom looked at us and said, "Me too"
It was the happiest moment of my life.

My Son is a Faggot

*Coming out being a rollercoaster, some people have
experienced the worst of it.*

It was my 14th birthday
The last time I saw or talked to my father.
I was just released from the hospital.
No, I'm not crazy
I got out with one concussion to my head
A fractured wrist
Bruising all over.
It wasn't self-inflicted.
I came out to my dad on my 14th birthday two days ago.
I guess that's his way of saying happy birthday.
My dad has never been a supporter of gay rights.
I knew this going into coming out.
I told him last because with him it would probably be the hardest
to do.
It was.
I don't remember a lot from what happened.
I just remember my mom screaming while she tried to stop him
And her taking me to the hospital.
I didn't tell anyone that it was my father that did this
I just said I slipped and fell down the stairs.
I don't think they believed me
But they didn't ask too many questions.
My mom just stayed with me the entire time.
And she told me on our way home she kicked my dad out
And he will not be there when I get home.

That's so GAY Fact #4

In June of 1970, the first pride parade was held
To commemorate the one-year anniversary of the
Stonewall riots in New York City

Pride parades are celebrated in most major cities nationwide
And many countries worldwide.

Despite the threat of the "Kill the Gays" bill
Looming in Parliament
And homosexuality being illegal
And punishable by up to 14 years in prison,
Uganda celebrated their first pride parade
In August of 2012

-Brydum
-Williams
-Wythe

PRIDE Month!

It's PRIDE month this month.
I cannot wait for pride festival!
I told my mom that I was going to Chicago
To stay with a friend for the festival
And she was excited for it but asked what it was all about
I explain it to her every year.

She asks if it is just what people post on Facebook,
AKA getting drunk and sleeping with people.

To everyone PRIDE is a different celebration.
For me PRIDE is a celebration of unity
Among the LGBTQA community.
I include "A" because of the Allies
Because it is not only for gay and lesbians and transgendered
people.
It's our whole community.
Pride is a pride in making it.

I honestly cannot think of a place with that much love
Love is everywhere in the air at PRIDE
I have met some extremely fun people at each PRIDE I've been
to.
PRIDE is about self-pride
It's saying together
I'm here
I'm strong
And I am making it
Living my life with whomever I love.

I've been out for 4 years
And have attended PRIDE for 3 years.

PRIDE isn't about getting drunk and finding Mr. Right Now,
It's about standing beside all the members
And allies of the LGBT community
Because we are the community
That is the most accepting of each other.

Yes, there are the people looking for the hook up
But its more about celebration that we,
As a community made it to another year
Closer to the human equality.

Memorial: They Paved the Way

Harvey Milk
Born May 22, 1930
Was the first openly gay man
Elected into a public office.
He started organizing against discrimination of gay and lesbian
rights in the Castro district in San Francisco
He was assassinated November 27, 1978
We remember him.

Matthew Shepard
Born December 1, 1976 became the face of hate crimes:
A student brutally murdered for being gay.
Matthew Shepard's murder brought national attention to hate
crimes.
He was always trying to better the world with acceptance of
people of any background.
He was beaten,
Robbed,
And left for dead
Tied to a fence.
He died in the hospital days later.
On October 12, 1998
He was only 21 years old
We remember him.

In 1969 the Stonewall riots took place at the Stonewall Inn in
New York.
The riots took place because
The police were enforcing a certain number of
Gender appropriate articles of clothing per individual.
The people at the inn rioted to protest this discrimination.
We remember those individuals.

Don't Ask Don't Tell was a policy that protected military
personnel
Against harassment of anyone
Who was closeted or bisexual,
While also banning openly gay,
Lesbian
And bisexual individuals
From joining military services.
If any person in the military was found to be gay
The grounds of Don't Ask Don't Tell
Would allow that individual
To be discharged from the military.
In 2011 President Obama signed a bill into law
To repeal the Don't Ask Don't Tell policy.
This now allows openly gay individuals
To serve in the military.
This was a landmark change in the LGBT Rights Timeline.
We remember this.

More heroes include

Beynard Rustin
Alan Turing
Gertrude Stein
Sylvia Rivera
Gloria Anzaldúa
Rita Mae Brown

All have paved the way
These individuals are the heroes of the past
Their legacy is remembered
Their legacy will never be forgotten
Their sacrifice for us today
We remember them
Among many more.
Who helped us get to where we are now

The Baddest Bitch

Drag now is highlighted in Pride Parades and festivals nation wide. While drag is a form of female impersonation, some people use drag to feel normal before they look into the change.

When I first meet people and they ask my occupation,
I tell them my day job
And then I tell them my night job is an entertainer.
They look confused then I tell them
I'm a drag queen.

The imaginative people can see it
But most people are still confused,
So I pull out my phone and show them a picture.
Then they are able to see the painted side of me.

When I am painted I am a party girl,
Flirty, friendly, and probably the baddest bitch!
Basically she has more balls then me.

When I'm out of face I'm actually pretty shy
I don't go to approach people too often
I'm pretty laid back

But going back and forth gets harder and harder
Because my character keeps getting more and more complex.
I'm a Gemini, which means that I have so much personality
I can have personality for me and for another person

So I created my drag persona

Or an alter ego.
There is a passion I have for doing drag.
I also enjoy going shopping for girly things.

I am what you call a fishy queen
Because I am all about being a girl in face,
And in all girl clothes.
There are multiple different types of queens,
Some, like myself are fishy queens,
There are comedy queens, show-girls
And then performance queens
To name a few.

I get a lot of people who ask me
If I am trying to be a girl in real life.
NO, not at all
I love being a boy,

But I also like doing girly things in drag.
At the end of the night I get out of face

I live as a boy during the day.
I am another person when I am in drag
And totally different when I am out of drag.

Doing drag is a way for me to feel like a girl
While being a boy.
I am a boy in drag.
My drag is being a female impersonator.

I have had some of the most amazing experiences by doing drag

I have been able to travel the country to perform.
I have also met some amazing people who find it unbelievable
That I look so beautiful painted
And can pull off being a girl,
But I am a boy in a dress.

When I am painted
I take all the feminity that I see
When I see women and all females.

One thing I can always say is my drag persona is always
Changing and discovering new things about herself,
But I will always know who I am and who she is
In face as well as out of face.
She is a part of my life as my alter ego
She can do anything she wants
Because she is a bad bitch

I'm just a straight guy with HIV

When I found out I had HIV I was only 16
I got HIV during my birth from my mother.
It was in the time when they didn't have a way to change that
Especially since HIV wasn't really known about.
I was told when I was younger
But never knew what it was about until now.

Now I have to take medications to help with it
They give me a chance to keep living.
Taking my medicines often makes me drowsy
and unable to function well after taking them.
Often there is an assumption that I asked for this disease,
By my alleged behaviors…
But I didn't have a choice.
I have never had sexual contact with another man.
I am a heterosexual man,
I was born with HIV
I didn't get it from being promiscuous.
So the misconception of me being a promiscuous male who
sleeps with males is not part of my life.
I have many friends who are gay and are HIV negative.
It is not something that people want,
The medicines are expensive,
They take a lot out of a person to just simply take them.
It is a rough lifestyle but I live each day with this.
I am not dying from this virus
I am living with this virus.

That's so GAY Fact #5

A recent study of LGBT youth
Who receive gay-sensitive HIV prevention education in school
Showed they engage in less risky
Sexual behavior than similar
Youth who did not receive such instruction

-GLSEN Gay, Lesbian, Straight education network

And Then He Was Gone

This paper will be the death of me.
I'm just trying to keep my life and emotions in check.
Writing this paper on Romeo and Juliet.
It's just a sad story.
It's about two people who love each other enough
to give up their lives for each other.

Basically the only question is rhetorical.
Is it better to have loved and lost,
Than never have loved at all?

I loved someone once.
4 weeks ago we celebrated our three-year anniversary
and I still break down at the simple sound of his name.
I still say he is my boyfriend.
I haven't deleted him from my phone
I can't even say his name.

Well it all started with him picking me up from school.
He had a stuffed tiger for me.
We went to my favorite restaurant.
Had dinner and went on a walk by the river.
After our walk he took me home.
I was on cloud 9 and nothing could bring me down.

Ok, I need to finish this paper.
It is better to have loved and lost
Because the feeling of true love is the highest of emotions I have
ever felt.

The feeling of love is the best feeling at the end of the day,
hearing his voice made me smile.

The phone rang
It was his mom crying.
She told me she was on the way to the hospital.
I asked if everything was okay?
She told me that he was in a car accident on his way home.
A drunk driver ran a red light and hit his car.
He was rushed to the hospital
She was on her way there now.
I told my mom to take me to the hospital
Because of what happened.
She dropped me off

I told her that his mom would take me home
Then I went to meet his mom.
She had just found out that there was internal bleeding
They had to operate on him immediately.
The doctor told us it wasn't looking good
But they would do their best.

After 2 hours of waiting
Praying
And hoping
The doctor came to talk to us.
He told us that they did their best
He didn't pull through.
His mom grabbed me
And sank to the ground crying.

She was basically a second mother to me.
She was the only one who knew we were dating.

I'm not out.
To everyone we were best friends
But we were dating.
I love him with all my heart.
He told his mom that I was the one.
We were young but I can say I was in love
We were together for a long time.

All I hear from psychologists is that
Time will heal and time will mend.
But if I knew it was going to be the last we were together
I would have held on to him longer.

No one understands what we had.
When school came up after the accident
Everyone was crying and told me that it's ok
We all lost a friend.

We did promise that we would be the last one to kiss each other's lips
And we were.

I love you babe!

The Day We Say, "I DO"

Same sex couples have the legal right to get married in nine states in the United States. Some states have different legislature that allow same sex civil unions.

Yes, I've been with him for about 14 years.
We got engaged at 6 years of being together.
We got engaged knowing that we weren't able to get married.
We agreed to get engaged because we knew that one-day
We would get married and it would be legal.

To us, marriage is more than a piece of paper
That means the world to us.

When he was taken into the emergency room after a car accident
last winter
I was unable to see him because we were not married.
All I want is to see this country that I pay taxes in,
That I could join the army to fight for,
Where I live and where I vote,
I am asking that this country would
Recognize me as an individual
And recognize the family that I want to create.

No, I do not see a difference between heterosexual and
homosexual partnerships.
Without a marriage certificate the government sees us as strictly
roommates.
We go on dates,
We make dinner,

We fight about dumb things
But most of all we care for each other.
We told our parents that we are engaged
And our families support us
As a couple
They are excited for when we can legally get married. How
would you feel if someone told you that you were unable to
marry the one you love?
I am not asking for religions to bless our marriage.
Marriage licenses are given by the state.

Marriage isn't just about the party,
The dancing,
And the cake.
It is about showing someone that you love them,
That you want to care for them,
That you want to be responsible for them.

If civil unions and marriages are equal,
Would you trade your marriage for a civil union?
We have to travel with our wills and legal documents.
I am a human being that wants to experience love
Just like you.
At the end of the day
Isn't love the only thing that truly matters?
Put yourself in someone else's shoes
When thinking about someone else's rights

YOU LEFT ME HERE
WITHOUT EVEN CARING!

Suicide is maybe a way out. But leaving behind everyone who cares about you can leave them in feelings of anger and sadness.

Do you know what you did to me that day?!?
Do you know what you did to US??
You changed my life forever.
You were so selfish.
I don't understand how ANYONE could be that selfish!
You didn't think of me! You didn't think of Teddy!
You didn't think of Nick!
You didn't think of ANYONE!

FEAR,
ANGER,
SHOCK,
BITTERNESS,
EXHAUSTION,
LOST,
CONFUSED,
SAD,
DEPRESSED,
OUTRAGED,
BROKEN,
LONELY,
 FORGOTTEN!
These are all of the emotions I felt at one time.

Do you know what happens
When someone feels all of these emotions at once?!
They cry till they have no more tears.
They can't sleep because of the nightmares.
They can't escape the pain.
They hurt so deeply that they eventually pass out!

You forgot me.
How could you?
If you only would have called me,
I could've helped you.
If I had only known how depressed you were
...you hid it so well.

How could you look up the instructions on how to break the
hearts of everyone around you?
How could you go to Wal-Mart and buy those ingredients?
How could you check into that hotel on February 18th?
How could you write those letters?
How could you mix that bonide lime sulfur and that muriatic
acid?

How could you tape off all the vents
and lie in the bathtub
and breathe it in without thinking about any of us!?

How could you commit suicide
when you had so many people who loved you?!?!

What depressed you so much
that you actually followed through with taking your own life?

I don't think I'll ever understand.

Do you even want to know what you've missed out on?
I've moved to Chicago and gone to college.
Cecilia's 6-year-old brother, Aaron, has become leukemia free.
Nick dropped out of school.
Steve's grandfather passed away,
Jake, Nick, and Jeffy are opening up a hookah bar and restaurant
in Jeffersonville.
And you weren't here to see any of that!

You promised me you would see me graduate!
You promised me you would come see me in Beauty and the
Beast
…and you weren't there.

You lied to me! How could you?
You were one of my best friends
…and I trusted you.

Now you're gone forever.

Do you know how many times I called your cell phone?
After you were gone
Just to hear your voice?

I don't think I've ever missed anyone so much in my life.

I wish I could just go back in time
and change things for you.

If I had known how you were feeling,
I would've fought so hard to save you.
All of us would have.

I think you knew that though,
And that's why you hid everything so well.
You knew we would stop you
And you didn't want to be stopped.

I just want to know
what was going through your head that day

Who told you that life wasn't worth the fight?
They were wrong! They lied
Now you're gone.
And we cried!

I think about it everyday
…What could I have done to save you
…But how do you save a life
That doesn't want to be saved?

That's so GAY Fact #6

25-40% of youth
Who become homeless each year
Are LGBT,
And the number is likely much higher

-Lambda Legal

It Gets Better

During the weeks after high school
While getting ready for college
Most of the things I worried about in school
Became nothing to worry about at all

When I was in high school and I was out
I got picked on, I got beat up, and I even lost friends.

Once I left high school
I went to college and people didn't look at me differently.
I lived in a dorm and I had the people on my floor
But if they didn't like me being gay,
Then we just didn't become friends
There were people in my classes that I could be friends with

I went to a state school
There were sixty-plus people in my classes

No one cared who I liked
And no one cared about where I came from
Or my past, I had a new start.

When I walked up to people
No one knew my highs, lows, or anything in my past
Unless I shared it with them.

All the people that put me down are gone
Or at least I don't see them often enough
For them to get to me.

There were a few people from my high school
That came to the same university.
The campus is huge,
And the people I care about I can see.

The bullies who bullied me
For being gay are not in my life anymore.
It is okay being who you are.

Gay Boy Rant

There are many stereotypes that people push onto members of the LGBT community.

I've never really experienced a time when being gay was an issue
or problem
Until I came out.
Once I came out I realized how much stigma there is with being
gay.
AIDS, Sluts, inability to commit,
And two men are "unfit" to raise a child.
One of the worst ones is the idea that
Being gay defines me.
Being gay is NOT something that defines me as a whole.
I am a man who happens to be gay.
Not a gay who happens to be a man.
When talking about human rights
We talk about all rights of a human
I am a human.
I breathe
I do the same things you do
The only difference is who I love
I deserve the right to give and receive love
To whom ever I choose.
Being gay is not something that defines me as a whole.
After coming out I realized all these Stereotypes among more.
More people will look at me and their assumption is that I am a
straight male but I'm not.
And when that happens most people's views of me change.

My only thing is that being gay doesn't change who I am as a person.
One of my friends told me that the only difference between being black and being gay is that you do not have to tell your parents you're black.
And it is true
But even being "black" is a race,
Which is created by society.
Society has created race
And when you boil down everything
What it means to be black is constructed into stereotypes
I feel that homosexuality is in ways the same
Yes,
Homosexual means that someone is sexually active with people of the same sex or gender.
But it does not change who someone is as a person.
Being gay has only made me a stronger person
Because of the things that I have gone through.
I have been abused both physically and emotionally
For something I can honestly not explain.

Homosexuality is in nature, which makes it natural right?!
Homosexual tendencies are in both plants and animals. Bottle nosed dolphins, elephants, lions and monkeys all practice homosexual activities.
Most homosexual activities are about pleasure,
More than procreation.
I think that there are too many people in the world to keep making more.

And lets bring up AIDS,

74

AIDS does not see sexuality
Just like it does not see race, gender, religion or income.
Yes, most males that have AIDS got it from homosexual contact
But most women that have AIDS got it from heterosexual
contact.
AIDS is first a syndrome,
Diagnosed by a doctor
Brought on by HIV
Which can be transferred by
And through anyone
End of story.

And my last point in this rant is to address the ludicrous
accusation that two men or two females cannot raise a child.
If you have seen The Lion King and realized how amazing it is,
Then you will know that two males can raise a child.
Timon and Pumbaa both raised Simba
And he grew up and fought his uncle to become king.

If you do not like the Disney cartoon reference
Then lets talk about Zach Wahls
He was raised by two committed women.
He made national news because of his speech about family
He has made himself known by showing that he is a regular
straight guy.

To not bring up another point but this recently happened
I was in the elevator and a guy bumped into me
And told me that he accidently bumped into me
And it wasn't intentional.
I thought nothing of it.

And he then went on to tell me that it meant nothing
And that he did not want to have sex with me.

HOLD THE PHONE! What?!
Just because I am gay does not mean I want every guy that walks
by on that card does every straight guy want every girl that walks
by?
NO. Exactly.
Don't flatter yourself. I have standards.

GAYYYYY

Ok so this is my time to say this word
This word has a lot of good things
And some bad things associated with it
Are you ready?
You don't look ready
….
Do you have an idea what word this may be?
I'll give you a hint
It might have been the hardest word to say
Ok.
Are you ready?
3
2
1
GAY.
That wasn't too bad was it?
Lets try it again
GAYYYYY
Ok I'm feeling a little better about it.
Is anyone feeling uncomfortable about it?
Ok lets say it a few more times
Gay, gay gay
Alright that's like 5 times
Here say it with me.
GGGGGGAAAAAAAYYYYYYYY
Can we spell it too?
Give me a G!
Give me an A!
Give me a Y!
What's that spell?
GAY!
Lets say it a few more times
Gay Gay
Gay Gay

Gay Gay gay gay gay gay
Gay gay
Gay gay
Gay
Gay gay gay
Gay
Gay Gay

(Have fun with it. Get people to say it with you. Sing it, act it.
Scream it.)

Alright, I feel like we have said it enough
You now realize there is nothing wrong with the word.
It doesn't change anything in a person

Complete: Head to Toe

I got a date for my surgery…
You know the big one…
The one below the belt…
Make another face like that!
Yes I'm excited!
And nervous…
At the end of it all
I will really be me.
I'm sick of having to explain this to everyone
I am a trans-man or a man to some,
Plain and simple.

The thing is
Ever since I was a child
I never felt like I was right with the gender I was "assigned."

It might have just been a hormone imbalance or whatever
I just never felt as though I was a girl
My mom always wanted a daughter who liked doing girl things.
Shopping, doing nails, dating boys, you know.
I tried dressing tomboy and felt right,
I got in trouble by my mom.
I felt as though I was a boy trapped in a girl's body.

In high school I liked a girl for the first time
And I brought her home to my family,
They didn't like it too much
They rejected the idea of me being a lesbian
 Thought it was a phase.

In college I began looking into "the change"
I met with a doctor
We talked about it and he put me on T
I went through counseling because it is a big emotional ride
From coming out to friends and family
To introducing them to Justin not Caitlyn.
Most of my friends slip up
Sometimes calling me Caitlyn
But it's a journey for them too.

Yes, I am really truly excited for this change in my life, leaving
Caitlyn behind
As a previous step
And introducing Justin into my life.
The first thought when I wake up
From the surgery will be that
I am complete from head to toe.

That's so GAY Fact #7

84% of LGBT youth
Report verbal harassment at school
Based on their
Gender identity and expression

-GLSEN Gay, Lesbian, Straight education network

I can't "choose", is that a problem?

I kinda like two people...
One is so hot and he makes my knees weak

The other is this girl.
I know she likes me,
We talked about it
But it is something taboo because
Usually people are supposed to like girls or boys.

I can say I like both
Both give me a fever.
I told my mom I like guys *and* girls
She said if you like both
Then just choose guys because it's normal.

But I can't choose
I find attraction in both sexes.
Not just guys and not just girls.

Most people think I'm just a sex fiend when I say I'm bi.
I'm not!
I like both guys and girls

I don't know who I will end up with in the end.
It could be a guy.
It could be a girl.

My biggest pet peeve

Is when I meet people and someone says they are bi
Then they say they are gay a few months later.
Which gives bisexual people no credit
Because you have to choose one or the other.

I honestly can't. I like both.
I am not attracted to the body parts.
Well I guess that
I just need to see who I like more in this case.

That's so GAY Fact #8

Research suggests that the age of "coming out" has been dropping in recent years.
Increased access to information and wider availability of support services for LGBT youth, particularly in urban areas, have provided greater opportunities for self-affirmation and socialization.

-Project Q

He Isn't Out... I am... We're dating...

So I'm dating this guy...
Well, seeing him.
We have been seeing each other for quite a while.
He's the quarterback of the football team.
When we first started seeing each other
It was always only when alcohol or drugs were involved.
It always hurt me knowing we could never be a public couple,
Knowing everyone in school sees me as "That" gay guy.

After a few months
I was able to get him sober and cleaned up
Now he doesn't have to be drunk or on something to do anything.
It is good knowing he doesn't have to be on something for him to love me.
The first time we did 'It' he said he loved me,
And then again each time after that.
He would tell me that he wants to be with me.

He was really concerned about coming out his father
Who is very anti-gay
His dad would flip shit.

I told him I loved him and I told him
That I was here to stay until he tells me to go.
So this is a secret
We would still meet up at night and spend time together.

This one time we met up at the park
We drove separately

We were in his car when someone broke the windshield…
It was his dad.
His dad had followed him and found us together.

His dad pulled him out of the car and started beating him.
His dad threw him on the ground
And punched him in the stomach repeatedly
I tried to jump in.
His dad shoved me away,
And went back to punching him in the stomach and in the face.
I screamed, 'You're hurting him!'
His father didn't say anything.
I tried to get between Ethan and his dad to take a hit.
But Ethan pushed me away and told me to get out of here.
I didn't want to
Then he told me "Get the fuck out of here"
I had to leave,
I was hesitant but I left….
There was nothing I could do
I tried.
And he told me to leave.

Two Dads

With same sex marriages becoming legal in states, the starting of a family is coming as well. Some states ban same sex couples from adopting while some allow it. The thought of starting a family and raising children brings great joy to a couple.

Today was a very exciting day.
We got our adoption approved for a 4-year-old boy.
He will be our son.
Craig will be very happy to hear!
It took a little longer to get approved
But we did it.
My family will be happy to know that after 17 years together,
After 3 years of trying surrogates and trying to adopt,
We will have more in our family besides our dog.
My mother asked if we want our son to be gay?
Heavens no!
Although being a gay individual has changed since we have been together
And the thought of family finally became possible.
I would never want him to be gay.
If he is, then he is
We will love our child for whoever or whatever he is.
After 17 years of being with Craig
I cannot wait to have our own family
With our son, Hunter.
I wonder how he will feel growing up with two dads.
I couldn't be happier for this

I'm Sorry

Coming out is an emotional part of one's life. Feeling alone and not having anyone to talk to can scare some young people to turn to suicide as a way out.

Dear Mom and Dad,
I love you both with all of my heart.
Recently I have not been able to talk to you,
About this problem I am having.
Since I was a baby,
I remember you saying you would always love me.
This problem with me is scary.
It's different.
I wake up each morning knowing I am different,
Not normal,
Damaged.
With the words of everyone around me saying
It's the "wrong kind of love"
"God hates Fags"
There's so much hate going around.
The only thing I hear is how wrong this is.
With this much hate
I can't see a brighter light
The hate is cloudy.
I am through lying to myself
I'm gay.
It is the hardest thing for me to say.
I hear the people at school say how wrong it is.
Hearing people make gay jokes about everything.
I'm the only one who is dealing with this at school.

I'm out-numbered by everyone.
I have only felt alone recently
Because of this problem of mine.
I'm sorry mom and dad
I tried to make myself feel better
But it has been hard, knowing that I'm alone in this world.
I love you both with all my heart.
I hope that me leaving will give you guys a better life
Without my problem
And me.
I want you to tell the whole family that I am sorry
For my problem.
I want all my friends to know
That I will be better now.
I believe that I will be in a better place.
Some people do not
Thank you,
For being the greatest mother and father I could possibly ask for.
I know I had no choice
But thank you.
Do not dwell on this
Please live your life.

I love you to the moon and back,
Jon.

That's so GAY Fact #9

LGBT individuals
Account for 30% of all
Suicides each year

-Lambda Legal

It was an emotional rollercoaster

Chris and I first looked into adoption
When we celebrated our 6-year anniversary.
We got the paperwork done,
and we waited until we found someone.

In Indiana the birth parents have 30 days
Once the paperwork is completed
After the child is born.
In those 30 days the parents can decide to raise the child.

Then we met Jasmine,
She was 18-years old
Recently graduated from high school and was taking time off of
school.
She was 3 months pregnant when we met her.
She really enjoyed getting to know us
We planned that we would adopt her child when it she born.

Jasmine asked us to help think of names for our daughter.
We asked for permission from Jasmine to name her Kristen Jo
It was the a mix of my mother's middle name, Kristen
and Jasmine's middle name.
We decided to name her Kristen Jo.
We all liked the name

Jasmine became part of our family
After we decided about names
We took her shopping for Kristen and for her.
She invited us to her grandparent's weekly Sunday dinner

We met more of Jasmine's family
They were very excited about Chris and I and Jasmine.

As the weeks passed

We took Jasmine to the doctor
We would hang out with her and her mother
And go out for dinner and movies.
It was like having a bigger family.
We all considered her part of our family.

She will always be Kristen Jo's mother
And will always be welcome to see her.
We want Jasmine to take Kristen to buy her first bra
And learn all the lady things that we can't teach her.

When Jasmine was due she called us telling us
Kristen hadn't dropped
She was not dilated enough
So the hospital would induce her.

We were at the hospital
Jasmine asked if Chris and I could be in the delivery room
With her mother.

Once Kristen was born
Chris was the first person to hold her

He gave her to Jasmine.
Jasmine held Kristen and fed her.
Our social worker came in with papers
For Jasmine to give us permission to adopt Kristen Jo.
At that point we are allowed to take her home with us.

Jasmine has the right to ask for Kristen back
Within 30 days of signing the paperwork.

In those 30 days is Thanksgiving,
We invited Jasmine and her family to join our families for
Thanksgiving.
We tried not to think of what would happen

If Jasmine took Kristen back on thanksgiving
But the thought was in our minds.

Our families were so happy to see Chris and I start a family
And happy to see such a strong connections
Between Chris and I and Jasmine.
We all shared a love for Kristen Jo.

On the 26th day of the waiting period
When we went to visit Jasmine with Kristen
She seemed distant
We were scared she would ask for Kristen back.

With a sigh of relief we made it to day 30.
We received a call from our social worker
She informed us that she just got off the phone
Jasmine completely waved her rights as mother to Kristen Jo.

Kristen is our daughter officially!

We had a baby shower for
Kristen and Jasmine to meet all our
Family and friends again.
Everyone welcomed Kristen and Jasmine into our family

She will be part of Kristen's family
As long as she wants to be.
We hope she wants to be around forever.

Kristen will know her mother and family.
We will show her how much we love her
Each and every day.
Knowing that we made it
Through the 30-day baby wait

We still have her.
We are celebrating her birthday this week
With Jasmine and her family.

Memorial: Unspoken Heroes

Unspoken heroes
They are the people
who we have gotten to know on an individual level.
Whether it is a friend,
coworker,
mother,
father,
sibling,
professor,
community activist
and the people that we don't even know their names.

Real people like a friend, who isn't afraid to tell his story and be
who he truly is. He is free of judgment and has this uncanny
ability to open up and make people feel comfortable. Even
though he has been through some really hard times he still keep
his chin up and use it to learn instead of being sad. He is very
admirable

One of my professors at school was so supportive of
EVERYTHING i did and was so passionate about teaching
he made me feel comfortable with exploring my sexuality
through my art

My supervisor,
he was basically the friend I needed when I came out.
He was the friend
The father figure when my father disowned me
He is an amazing person
He is straight
Married
But he knew how to make me open up to him
He never pried
He just let me talk and he listened.

He accepted me for who I am
We still keep in contact because he was there for me

My sister is my hero.
She was there for me when I first came out
She gave me a hug
She told me she loved me for the first time
When I told the rest of my family
She was right there to support me.

The Hereafter

The Unspoken Monologues are a work in progress until there is equality for all.

These monologues are only some stories.

Each individual has a story to share.

Each story is different and each story deserves to be told.

This will be an ongoing movement for each person to tell a story.

If you have a story you would like to share please feel free to email me, as I will continue to write monologues for future volumes for the unspoken monologues.

UnspokenMonologues@gmail.com

Author's Note

When I look at my life, I see a river. Forever changing by the passing boulders, trees, rocks and even each grain of sand at the bed of the river. Each object, changing me and helping me keep moving. I came out after a semester at college and was accepted by mostly everyone. I visited my sister for her graduation from UIS the following May. We stayed up late talking and this idea for the monologues that came into my head after talking about *The Vagina Monologues*. I thought about the people I met in school, and thought about each person's story.

Everyone has a story to tell. I shared my idea for *The Unspoken Monologues* and they loved it. I began speaking to more people about their experiences and began writing.

The opening quote of this book inspired me because it exactly encapsulates my message. This is the mark I would like to leave on the world. Throughout the process of writing this show I learned about myself and about other people's lives. These stories are not casual stories. It has been an emotional process to interview people and talk about their experiences and how they have learned to cope.

I want to share this with the world. My one simple request is that if you would like to perform this show with your organization, please donate your proceeds to an LGBT organization in your area.

Every person's story is unique and their own. Out of respect for each personal story and every shared story, I request that any performance be a readers' theatre to stay true to each individual's story.

Thank you's

First I would like to thank each person that shared a story with
me.

I would like to thank my family
For being there for me,
Supporting me though coming out
and helping to edit this project of mine.

Also a thank you to each
Boulder,
Tree, and rock
In my river of life.

Gay Facts References

Brydum, Sunnivie. "Ugandan Parliament Reconvenes, With Lingering 'Kill The Gays' Bill." *Advocate.com*. Here Media Inc., 7 Feb. 2013. Web. 10 Mar. 2013.

United Nations. "World Humanitarian Day 2012 - Behind The Scenes with Beyoncé" Video. *Youtube*. Youtube, August 17, 2012. Video. Retrieved: February 15 2013.

Williams, Steve. "LGBT Ugandans Show Their Pride Despite Risk." *Care2.com*. Care2, 8 Aug. 2012. Web. 10 Mar. 2013.

Wisconsin Coalition Against Domestic Violence. "LGBT Youth Facts/Stats". (http://www.wcadv.org/sites/default/files/resources/LGBT%20Youth%20Facts%20and%20Stats.pdf). Retrieved: February 11, 2013.

Wythe, Bianca. "American Experience: TV's Most-watched History Series." *PBS.com*. Public Broadcasting System, 9 June 2011. Web. 10 Mar. 2013.

www.ingramcontent.com/pod-product-compliance
Lightning Source LLC
Chambersburg PA
CBHW030350290526
45785CB00004B/1681